Merry
Christmas 2010!

Laughing at Wine

Stephanie-
Thanks for managing
Through The Burnsville
closure, staffing challenges,
+ still succeeding with
retention efforts! -Andrew

Library of Congress Cataloging-in-Publication Data
Morris, Jerry
Laughing at Wine
ISBN 978-0-615-38475-7

Self published by "Laughing at Whatever LLC"
www.laughingatwhatever.com

For Joy

for the years searching you
for the years since
for kids and pets
for years hence

"They call me the wine whisperer."

Praise for the Author, Jerry Morris

"After reading this book wine now tastes funny."

Chris K. of New Ulm, MN.
Unemployed Edsel mechanic

"Mr. Morris had to sample a lot of wine in order to write this book."

Luverne of New Ulm, MN.
Part time hair dresser specializing in bluing gray hair.

"Darla makes me feel better about myself. Her advice gives me goose bumps."

Wanda of New Ulm, MN. Recently released St. Cloud Reformatory for the clinically insane majoring in eye contact and the many uses of a toothbrush. (degree pending)

"It's duck bumps dearie."

"Mr. Morris use to be a famous Leisure Consultant until the pressure got to him."

Fred aka Fifi Lanude of New Ulm, MN. Janitor specializing in unisex bathrooms.

"Do you think Fred is a cross dresser?"

"Something's crossed."

"Darla, do you think this author is an idiot or a fool?"

"It's difficult to tell an idiot from a fool until both are drunk. Then it's always the fool who tries to guess which one of them is the idiot."

"I've always lived up to my billing."

Acknowledgements

Creator of Darla & Lloyd - Caroline Morris who said, "Daddy, if this book is successful can we start a distillery in Colorado?"

Advisor & Creative consultant- Kendall Morris who said, "Dad, if this book is successful can we rescue even more animals?"

Advisor, Creative consultant and Proof reader - Dick Martin who said "Jerry, your idioms are redundant."

"What are idioms?"

"Sayings by idiots."

Advisor & Creative consultant - Joy Morris who said "I do" 23 years ago and more recently "honey, if this book is successful will that mean you have a job?"

Artist / Illustrator - Emmy Award winner Joel Seibel, who is rumored to be madly infatuated with Darla. It's sad to see a man of his caliber fall so low.

Marketing - Julie Stokes who said "print it and they will come." That's why she is the best.

Web Designer - Taylor Brink, who said his processor's floating point unit performs at 70 gigaflops. He must be a very happy man.

Book cover envisioned by Joy Morris

Book cover created by Pierre Renoir & Joel Seibel.

Graphic Designer - Rachel Rice who said, "Jerry you may need a lot more help than I possibly can give you. Here is the number of a good psychiatrist."

"My psychiatrist gave me the nicest compliment today. He said I'm an egoMEniac."

Advisor - Dave Hinman, who must have said "there's no number big enough that you can't add two more zeros to it."

And a Special Thanks to Andrea George who is Darla in real life

"I'm a wine connoiSEWER."

Introduction

I never knew wine could be so funny, so intimate, so revealing, so much like life itself. Yet the more I talked with wine lovers the more I realized wine is a world unto itself. The humor, superstition, rituals and language surrounding wine are fascinating. My mind began a free association meander that didn't stop until this book was completed (or rather when I was fed up with it).

Darla is the perfect logo for "Laughing at Wine." She makes you laugh as she waddles throughout the collective consciousness of the wine drinker seen through the blurry eyes of the author.

This book is nonfiction, fiction, autobiographical, text and a comic book all rolled into a satire (whatever that is), for your personal reading and drinking pleasure.

"Laughing at Wine" is best read under the influence and should be hidden from impressionable children, if in fact there are any impressionable children left in this world.

"I'm impressionable around NFL running backs."

And the best part is you get to write the next book! I can't possibly think of anything else to say. Actually I took Darla's advice when writing this book. She said if I needed witty comments and funny quotes I should track down a forty something year old Englishman who still lives with his mother. And ask the mother. Well that's exactly where all the humor came from but since then the bloke moved out. So I'm asking you to write me humorous stories or comments about wine. Just go to www.laughingatwine.com. More about that later.

My goal for writing this book (other than paying for good moonshine) is to help us understand life is tragic, insufferable, pathetic, fallible, out of control and delightful if you love yourself. And laughing at yourself and your predicament in life with a glass of wine in hand reinforces the accurate concept that you're not perfect "so get use to it everybody."

Darla and Lloyd are the funny side of each of us and they'll be a reminder that we are doing the best we can. Also, drinking a glass of tasteful wine is like a quiet toast to oneself. "I celebrate me." "I got up this morning, fed the kids some cereal junk, flipped off one guy on the way to work, made a few good decisions and one real boner, was hostile to only one co-worker at a time, cheated on weight watchers, fed the kids a hot supper (the pizza man is close), kissed my dog and hugged the husband before turning in (or maybe I hugged the dog and kissed my husband-doesn't really matter). What more can you ask for? So celebrate and laugh with Darla, Lloyd and others.

"I want to be an enigma."

Choosing Wine

I spend two or three days a week at a wine store helping people choose suitable wines. The reasons they often choose one bottle over another are complex, illogical and humorous. Listed below are a few funny selection criteria.

"It's the same color as my carpet, just in case I throw up."

"Turning the bottle just so with some light in the background you can see Jesus wearing a little crown of thorns."

"Of all the wines you have in the store this one tastes best after tequila shots."

"When my wife goes through PMS I always buy her wine that has a goat on the label."

"This Chardonnay goes well with Shrimp. My husband is only five feet tall you know."

"My roommates hate this one so I'll take three bottles."

"I won't drink wines from Australia. I met my ex-husband there."

"My husband calms down after I drink a bottle of Red Blend."

"If I can't pronounce it I ain't drinking it."

"It tastes good on the rocks."

"This brand of Merlot tastes just bad
enough to give the impression it's
expensive."

"I need a box wine to place on the top
shelf of my shower."

"A vintner took me in his wine cellar. I couldn't help myself, he had a bed and candelabras down there"

" Darla, do you know the five food groups?"

"Yea, red wine, white wine, caffeine, sugar and fat."

"I met the owner of the vineyard that produces this wine. He was an ass. I'll take a case."

"This Chianti is exquisite through flavored straws."

"I get so confused sometimes and this Shiraz clears my palate."

"I blend this Pinot Gris with aloe and pear juice for a quick pick me up first thing in the morning."

This Chardonnay compliments my scrambled eggs.

"During a séance my dead mother in law appeared and told me to drink plenty of this Sonoma Valley Blend. It's quite a coincidence that it is one of my favorites."

You think I'm kidding. I'm not. Actually there were several other reasons people choose certain wines but they were all X rated. Share with us your secret reasons for choosing wines.

" It has alcohol in it?"

" Did I mention I'm an egoMEniac?"

Facts, Definitions & Insights

We're making so much progress already. You've learned people choose wines for various reasons and you can't depend on others for guidance, not even those who drink several bottles a day. So choosing wines that fit your palate and budget can be a lone and scary decision. I may be able to help.

Wine knowledge can be invaluable when choosing wines. You've come to the right place. Listed below are a few often misunderstood terms and facts about wines that will boost your confidence. Only by studying these can you encompass the author's true perspective on wine and get a titillating glimpse into his unique lifestyle.

" *It's obvious this author is full of Gewurztraminer!*"

Basic wine knowledge

A grape is a fruit that grows on perennial woody vines. (This is a good start don't you think? Even the insane can act sane in the beginning.)

" I knew a Drake that had a perennial woody."

Recent archeological digs have strongly suggested wine production actually began some 8500 years ago in Georgia. I visited that very region once while driving from Macon to Atlanta.

Basic wine knowledge

White wine is neither white nor comes from white grapes. It's golden color is determined by the fermentation and aging process.

White grapes are actually different shades of green and are a mutant of the red grape.

" My girlfriend called me a mutant. I took it as a compliment."

"Terrain" is a word often used to describe the many subtle influences on a grape. Such as:

ELEVATION OF THE VINEYARD

ASPECT TO THE SUN OR SLOPE OF THE LAND

THE MOOD AND NATIONALITY OF THE GRAPE PICKERS

WHETHER THE VINTNER IS HAPPILY MARRIED OR NOT

THE MOON PHASE ON DATE OF HARVEST

SEASONAL RAINFALL

TYPE AND CHEMISTRY OF THE SOIL

THE SEXUAL ORIENTATION OF THE VINTNER.

"*I like facing east when having sex.*"

"*Up is my best orientation.*"

The most important influence on a grape is the music the pickers were singing during harvest. For example:

DELTA BLUES
Produces a rather somber Pinot Noir

BLUEGRASS
Causes jug wines to literally bounce off your palate till you whine with enthusiasm

" I always hum The Star Spangled Banner when having sex."

" I yodel!"

Jazz
Gives red blends a litany of flavors
without a dominant note

Inspirational Gospels
Embrace a chorus of aromas that often
bring you to your knees

Country
Produces a twangy Merlot with a flinty
finish

Rock and Roll
Produces acidic Sauvignon Blancs that
defy any conventional boundaries

Below are a few misunderstood wine terms.

WINE SNOB:
One who knows wine better than he knows himself.

NOSE:
What one sticks into a glass and pronounces "it smells like—well wine."

" If I stick my nose in too far it causes my mascara to gum up."

WINE BORE:
One who knows wine better than he knows you.

PALATE:
What's too stupid that it has to be educated to enjoy wine.

" My palate is larger than most."

WINO:
One who knows wine better than he knows himself or you, caring for neither party an iota.

BOUQUET:
The melding of musk aftershave, scents from a poorly rinsed facial masque, the aroma of a $40 bottle of $12 Chardonnay and too much Arid Extra Dry on a first date at a wine bar.

FINISH:
The taste one has in his mouth after drinking a full bottle of wine on an empty stomach. "

AERATION:
The same as airation except airation is not a word.

AMBIANCE:
More expensive than atmosphere but cheaper than milieu.

WINE BARS:
UPC code on the back of wine bottle.

BALANCE:
What one hopes for on the way to the restroom after completing the "finish.

" *I have great balance, webbed feet.*"

DOM PERIGNON:
A guy who could sell a lot more Champaign in America if he'd change his name to Don.

COMPLEX:
Much like a complex child. You don't know if he is brilliant or undesirable.

NOBLE ROT:
What happens to important people when they begin to believe they deserve their good fortune.

HONEYED:
Past tense of honey, meaning after your girlfriend left you.

ADULTERATED WINES:
Once consumed these wines allow you to fantasize about having sex with someone other than your spouse.

" My favorite varietal."

FULL BODIED:
How you feel after the wrong choice of wine gives you indigestion.

ICE WINE:
Created when a lazy vintner dragged his sorry ass in such a manner that assured his failure in harvesting his grapes before they froze. Having less juice he raised the price and named it "Ice Wine," voila!

BRANDY:
The choice of wine drinkers in a rush.

PISSE VIN:
A wine I wouldn't drink unless I personally watched it bottled and corked.

" Getting corked is absolutely no fun, but getting uncorked is another thing altogether."

KOSHER WINES:
The bottles with a little Torah cookie attached to it.

JUG WINES:
Enterprising wineries attempting to corner the hillbilly market.

GRENACHE:
The act of chewing wine as you drink it.

SMOKY:
The taste your wine develops after a drunken party guest furtively flicks cigarette ashes into your glass of Pinot Noir.

ROOM TEMPERATURE:
Anywhere from 55 degrees to 85 degrees depending on which particular life phase you are presently experiencing.

TOASTY:
A two glass predecessor to toasted.

CHARACTER:
A term often used to describe a wine or person that you dislike but are in a position where it's prudent not to be truthful. As in "this wine has character," or "he is a real character."

EARTHY:
Similar to character but worse.

TART:
A woman who drinks wine with anyone who'll buy.

TUSCANY:
A bunch of rocky hills in Italy that American wives often mention when complaining to their husbands about the lack of romance in their marriage.

" What's the difference between sex and love?"

" *$200 and some rope.*"

PROVENCE:
Areas in France that have no particular importance except to the people who can't pronounce Provence.

GRAPE CONCENTRATE:
What a person suffering from Attention Deficit Disorder can accomplish after drinking enough wine.

PH:
Personal heartburn.

LUSH:
The description of the lips of the woman you just served a hearty red to.

CORKAGE:
The precise amount it would take to shut up a wine bore.

LIMPED:
In the wine tasting world it describes a wine that is crystalline, luminous and bright. In the real world no man would knowingly drink a limped wine.

DEPTH:
How much of the bottle you drank.

" I'm a superficially deep person."

BOONES FARM:
Earnest and Julio's gallant attempt at
volunteer prohibition.

Understanding these wine terms now in
a different light will dramatically change
your wine drinking experience.

I encourage you to write me if there
are wine related terms you don't
understand. More importantly, if you
have "nontraditional" insight into some of
wine's terminology please share it through
our website and we will share it with our
readers.

Just go to www.laughingatwine.com.

"Ta-Da!"

" I'm not a cheap drunk but I'm cheaper drunk."

Second Brain

Your confidence must be soaring. Few people other than students of this book really understand wine. The previous chapter sets you apart from casual wine drinkers. No longer will you suffer the arrows of embarrassment because you lack wine knowledge.

Often when I expound on my wine expertise people just up and leave the conversation from pure intimidation I'm sure. Soon you'll be able to impress people just like the author.

Now let's discuss using price as a selection criteria. Is a $60 bottle of wine 3 times better than a $20 bottle?

" Only if the cork gets popped"

No! The answer is no.

Price points often reflect wine ratings. Ratings are subjective and bestowed by "wine experts" whose palates are probably far different than yours. Remember one's palate reflects one's background and experiences. Until you find that expert who shares a similar background you must depend on your first and second brains to make informed choices.

You may ask where or what is your second brain? I'll give you a hint. It's neither your spouse nor your sexual apparatus.

" My first brain is definitely my stomach."

Mr. Michael Gushon wrote a very erudite book on the second brain creatively naming it "The Second Brain." He explains what ancient man knew and trusted and modern man has chosen to ignore.

Your second brain is your gut! In short the neurological make up of your gut is similar to your first brain unlike any other part of your body.

Our first brain (the one in your skull) must honor and acknowledge the second brain before the gut can work. And there's the rub. We often do not listen to our feelings, consequently rationalizing through decisions. And as we know rationalizing is modern man's way of lying to himself honestly.

"Each morning I choose the sweetest lie to live the day by."

Actually, integrating your first and second brains is freeing and funny. Otherwise you become fact smart but a practical moron.

"I use my emotions to celebrate and my logic to post bail."

Similarly the left and right hemispheres of the first brain have to work together before we become a whole thinking human. Obviously this applies whether you're choosing a mate or selecting a wine for dinner. Look at all the idiotic decisions politicians, celebs, athletes and others make. They obviously weren't thinking with both brains.

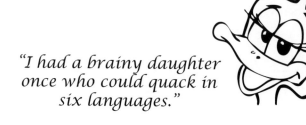

"I had a brainy daughter once who could quack in six languages."

English: quack, quack

French: quache`

Italian: quackederci

Japanese: quackamoto

German: quoc!

Spanish: equackarilla

I'd like to hear your second brain, or lack of second brain, stories.

"I love, therefore I believe in God."

"I make love, therefore I believe in heaven."

"I bear children, therefore I believe in retribution."

"I divorce, therefore I believe in Satan."

"I drink wine and laugh, therefore I believe in me."

"*The journey from lust to depravity is but a waddle*"

Reasons Palates Change

Your digestive system communicates chemically to both brains. It strives to find balance between a narrow PH range and still enjoy a variety of taste sensations. An imbalance in the stomach is relayed to taste buds and olfactory glands thereby changing which foods and drink are presently desirable. Taste and smell are windows into the status of one's second brain. Honor them!

You wouldn't eat disagreeable food and neither should you drink unpleasant wine regardless of their cost or rating.

But it is important to remember outside events can alter digestive balance quickly. An argument with your daughter, for example, can send you straight to a previously unappealing bottle of Chardonnay.

" Children are a sign of life, but so is a panic attack."

Even personal viewpoints or private musings may cause a significant change in your palate. To help you more readily recognize these palate altering events I've listed a few that my family and friends have experienced.

Everyday Reasons Palates Change

Your Grandma rolled her stockings down below her knees in front of you and your new friends.

You saw your daughter on TV waving to the camera during an episode of "Lesbians Gone Wild."

Your daughter, in above example, called and asked you to break the news to her fiancée.

Your son struck out three times at his last baseball game; and it was T-ball.

" I seldom strike out."

Your personal psychic was killed in a plane accident.

" *My psychic died of an over active premonition.*"

Bought an entertainment center from
IKEA.

For three weeks now your TV has been
setting on the box the entertainment center
came in.

Having to explain to your pre-school
provider why your 3 year old daughter has
such a foul mouth.

Spending way too much time wondering why people heed the advice of a man named Confucius.

Realizing that if you had known the difference between aspect and aspic your horoscope would have been more meaningful.

Having your third first date this month.

Being proud of your daughter who failed 10th grade algebra just like you did 20 years ago.

Realizing the left over bacon you ate this morning was your dog's beggin strips.

You live in Minnesota and the farmer at the outdoor market sold you his expensive homegrown bananas.

You got fired from your volunteer job.

Your defense lawyer tells you he's
convinced you're guilty.

Somehow feeling better about salvation
when you realize God just might be female.

Being happy that our bodies don't go with us when we die.

Wondering if it's too late to change the first names of your teenage children.

Realizing it took one child two months to instill in you the virtues you rejected for 25 years in church.

"Truthfulness and romance seldom sleep together. That's why I never accept a date from an honest man."

Realizing that in the last two years your neutered female dog has humped more things than you have.

" I'd like her cell number."

You've had four soulmates this year already.

People are starting to call you ma'am.

Realizing that you actually know the exact
number of ceiling tiles in your bedroom.

Getting so old that the gender of your sex partner is becoming less and less important.

"Old age occurs the moment your virtues become more regrettable than your vices."

Wondering why the bust of a person also includes their head and neck.

Your talking scale refuses to speak for fear of reprisal.

Realizing the historical impact Campbell's Cream of Mushroom Soup has made on the Lutheran Church.

Wondering what kind of parent you have been when your youngest child's career goal is to open a distillery.

Trying to reconcile the fact that people less fortunate and less deserving than you are having a lot more fun in life.

Finding fun ways to stay within
the Weight Watchers point system.
For example:

1st day   3 ½ bottles red wine   24 points

2nd day   2 ½ bottles red wine
                                            >   24 points
            1 package Twinkies

3rd day   2 ½ bottles white wine
                                          > 24 points
            1 package Little Debbies

4th day   3 ½ bottles red wine   24 points

5th day   2 ½ bottles red wine
                                          >   24 points
            1 package soft Purina   estimated
            cat food

6th day   3 bottles red wine

½ bottle white wine $>$ 24 points

pickle juice

7th day   1 bottle red wine

2 hospital meals $>$ Indeterminate points

2 bags glucose taken intravenously

Tell me what changes your palate!

"I'm a hall of fame member of the mile high club."

Sex & Wine

Drinking wine has so many similarities to other aspects of life. It occurred to me that the interrelationship between drinking wine and sex are inseparable. At first glance one wouldn't expect them to have very much in common but take a look at these below.

Similarities Between Sex and Drinking Wine

THEY ARE BOTH DELICIOUSLY EVIL
YET CURIOUSLY STILL LAWFUL.

YOU CAN PARTICIPATE IN EITHER
ACTIVITY ALONE OR WITH
OTHERS.

THEY BOTH CAN BE DONE IN
ALMOST ANY POSITION OR
LOCATION YET NEITHER SHOULD
BE DONE WHILE DRIVING.

YOU USE YOUR LIPS.

THE MORE YOU PAY FOR IT THE
GREATER THE DISAPPOINTMENT.

"I give a baker's dozen."

HAVING EITHER MAKES YOU WANT TO LAUGH ALBEIT FOR DIFFERENT REASONS.

NEITHER ACTIVITY IS SO ENJOYABLE THAT IT CAN'T BE RUINED BY WATCHING 30 MINUTES OF REALITY TV.

HAVING ENOUGH OF EITHER TEMPORARILY RIDS YOUR LIFE OF WORRIES.

FOREIGN ONES HAVE A SPECIAL ALLURE.

"C'est La Vie, sailor."

YOU'RE NEVER SO OLD THAT YOU DON'T THINK YOU CAN HANDLE MORE THAN YOU'RE GETTING.

You have sex to produce children and drink wine to make them disappear.

You can enjoy both on the dining room table.

Too much of either can make you lightheaded.

They both are improved with your clothes removed, preferably by someone else.

The more wine drunk the better sex remembered.

Both wine and sex can be purchased from the Internet.

"*www.wineandwhine.com.
My personal one stop
shopping Mecca.*"

You replace the lack of either with food.

You lie about the quality and quantity your getting.

POPCORN DOESN'T SUIT EITHER
ACTIVITY BUT A JAR OF CREAMY
PEANUT BUTTER DOES.

WHEN EITHER SEX OR DRINKING
WINE GO POORLY ONE USUALLY
ENDS UP IN THE BATHROOM.

"Bathrooms are for quitters."

THE CHOICE OF COLOR IS THE EASIEST DECISION.

"Once you've had yellow you stay mellow."

Do you have other sex vs. drinking wine comparisons? You must! All of the above are from my personal experience, or lack of experience. You can use a pseudonym name.

"Never underestimate a strip search."

Just Enough

Ducks and Hounds as well as most other animals know happiness is having just enough. But just enough is not a concept well accepted or even understood by humans.

It's probably a DNA thing.

"What's DNA stand for?"

"Darla's
Natural
Attributes
I'm full of it."

Man imagines happiness as a linear function with a limitless goal. We assume bigger and better are pathways to fulfillment. This erroneous concept filters down to the smallest and most trivial daily decisions, even to our choices about food and drink. It goes something like this. If two glasses of wine taste wonderful and makes you feel warm and confident it goes without saying four will double your feelings of well being, eight might bring you near ecstasy while sixteen might evoke nirvana herself etc. Reality would suggest the following instead.

"Reality is not what it's cracked up to be."

Two glasses of wine make you feel warm and slightly lightheaded. You're not so uptight about how well your dinner party is being received or if the guests are enjoying themselves. "They need to be responsible for their own fun."

"It's darn near impossible to get uptight when you have a short attention span."

Your husband is being the perfect cordial host. Your dress is a little snug, you had hoped to be 5 pounds lighter by now but it just didn't happen. For some reason your two teenage children have chucked their normal morose attitude for a sickening sweet demeanor. And the guests are complimentary of the house and food. The evening seems to flow.

After four glasses of wine you begin to converse more easily with your guests although their responses seem inconsequential.

"Inconsequential, my middle name."

Your husband appears overly friendly to one particular guest who happens to be single and thin. You suspect your children have been pilfering liquor because they appear both giddy and stoned simultaneously. The thinner guests ignore their entree in lieu of salad. The house seems cramped and hot. Your dress pinched in several tender places when you descended on hands and knees to blot up your spilled wine from the dirty carpet.

"I'm fortunate to be tender in lots of places."

After eight glasses you had the courage to confront your husband about his adulteress actions and admonish the kids for being little drunken thieves. Most of the guests declined dessert so in a fit of anger and anxiety you inhaled three thick slices of key lime pie upon returning them to the kitchen.

"I don't stop eating till my bellybutton goes from an inny to an outie. It's just like a little meat thermometer."

The house became so warm you opened all the windows and unbuttoned your ugly outdated dress. Many guests had the nerve to leave without so much as a goodbye.

After 10 glasses you punched Kitty Sorenstan. Her head was harder and nails sharper than you anticipated and your husband looked helpless for the first time since the birth of your first child.

To your surprise the cops were kinder than the doctors.

You faintly recall the kids taking lots of pictures for their new website, www.lookatmomgo.com.

But your memory was adequately intact to know that you would rather throw up in your own toilet than down town. You get the message. It's important to know when "just enough" has been exceeded. To help you recognize this invaluable yet elusive state I've listed a few incidents that might hint at one's overstepping "Just Enough."

YOU'VE EXCEEDED JUST ENOUGH WHEN

* When you start laughing at a joke long before the punch line is delivered.

*You mistake the can opener for the cork screw and complain that it's bent.

" I like losing sometimes. Then I get to drown my sorrows."

*You start combing your hair with your fake nails.

*Only after seeing your name and cell number scrawled on the stall door do you realize you are in the men's restroom.

*Sneaking from said restroom you cannot resist staring at the men standing at the urinals.

*Although humiliated by above transgression you are compelled to share the incident with other people in the restaurant.

*You can't read your grocery list.

*An hour before dinner guests are to arrive you decide to change the color of your hair.

*You have trouble remembering the ages of your children and say things like "I know how old they use to be."

*You enjoyed the last conversation with your mother.

*Your daughter's friends call you a cool mom.

"I want people to call me enigmatic."

*You actually agreed with your 15 year old son when he said school sucked.

*Halfway through the party you decide to turn your dress into a backless one.

*You become emotional when listening to Barry Manilow.

"Did I mention I use emotions to celebrate and logic to post bail."

*Too many high fives.

"There's never too much high anything. High butt, high heels and high breasts."

"Highballs, high cheeks bones, high high. All good."

*You have a strong desire to arm wrestle.

*For a brief moment you thought you were married to your first husband.

*Mistake the smoke alarm for the oven timer.

*You want to sing "Home on the Range" at Wed. night karaoke.

"I want to sing Hey Big Spender."

*You use the family Lhasa Apso to dust the mantel.

*You decide the solution to yesterday's problems is tomorrow.

*And the specific solution to your drinking problem is a bigger wine glass.

Whether you call it being drunk, plastered, corked, put to bed with a shovel, hammered, a wee tipsy, cancelled, juiced, legless, pickled, whiffled, plotted, stewed, tanked, fried, boiled as an owl, capsized, crispy, a skin full, upholstered, winterized, over served, all in a heap, diddled, teched, tittled, two thirds kicked in the ass, up a stump, waxed, zippered, above par, coagulated, amiably incandescent, awash, beautifully lit, scuppered, stocious, been to Jericho, behind the juice, chasing the duck, pished, plootered, puggled or redirected— it's not pretty. You are not wiser, sexier or improved in any way. Always watch for JUST ENOUGH.

"Once you've had yellow you never go back. Hey the truth doesn't always rhyme!"

Intoxicated Words & Phrases

There are some 400 English words and phrases in use today describing the state of intoxication. Since mentioning a few colorful ones in the last chapter I have had numerous requests to shed light on their origin. Our Drunk research panel was able to provide background material on the following ones.

PLOOTERED:

A descriptive word founded by Irish wives in the 16th century to describe inebriated husbands, who after a belly full of their country's best whiskey, would stagger home with lovemaking on their minds but with precious little follow through in their trousers. PLOOTERED is a marvelous unity of the words Plural and Neutered which indicated that the only thing that was about to rise that evening for these lassies was their ire.

"I always rise to the occasion, when the occasion rises."

PISHED:

A poignant yet revealing adjective formally recognized in 1898 which was uttered by the inebriant himself in a pitiful attempt to describe his present state of annoyance. That is, he's trying to say he's pissed, not that anyone cares. But the tongue being somewhat of a thicker grade at times like these falls clumsily from the front upper palate to sadly languish behind the lower front teeth preventing only a pathetic stab at the word pissed. "I'm pished" is usually their best attempt but most likely not their only attempt. For whatever reason and to our great relief pished people seldom try to incorporate words like penchant, thistle, exacerbate, listless, pussy chat or prostate in their conversational vocabulary that evening.

"A man's childishness is only as tolerable as he is rich."

BOILED AS AN OWL:

Is a uniquely American phrase specifically originating from the Panhandle region of Texas during the depression years. During those bleak and meager times these hardy people tried numerous ways to cook owl with only one rather humorous success. The resulting recipe instructed the cook to boil the owl for 10 min in a large vat of liquid made up of equal parts water and grain alcohol at the end of which one throws away the owl and drinks the broth. In other words if you are Boiled as an Owl you are essentially worthless even to those who had great hopes for you in the beginning.

OVERSERVED:

Is a self evident and revealing modern adjective often used by irresponsible drinkers who coincidently utter things like: "I didn't think she would get pregnant," or "I told the cop I was hurrying home because I shouldn't be driving in my condition."

TECHED:

17th century Englishmen described a mentally unstable person as "touched" by whom or what is mere speculation at this point in history. But it was but a small step to morph from touched to teched when depicting a person temporarily insane due to the juice of iniquity. Simply, if you're touched you're crazy and if you're teched you're crazy drunk.

TWO THIRDS KICKED IN THE ASS:

Was born by Scots circa 1650. This enigmatic phrase has confused our Drunk experts for years, one half attributing the 2/3 rds to the act of kicking and the other half the 2/3 rds to the ass itself. So we may surmise that either the drunken Scotsman could not kick his drinking buddies, or for that matter, himself in the arse with a fully delivered blow or the poor laddie at the end of a night of consumption appeared to have somewhat less of an ass for his mates to kick than when this otherwise innocent evening began.

BEEN TO JERICHO:

Although Jericho is a Palestinian city this colorful phrase was first used by a Scotsman in Aberdeen who was up on his geography. It was quickly picked up by surrounding communities and eventually the whole country because it so aptly represents the worst of all drunken conditions. You see, Jericho is only ten miles north of the Dead Sea and is the lowest permanently inhabited site on earth. Yes my fellow inebriants if you've "been to Jericho" you have been so low and pitiful, without mercy or sympathy, suffering hell on earth while the juice extracts its payment.

MAGOOGLED:

There are few things in life more personally revealing than our favorite childhood cartoon. During the fifties Columbia Pictures released 53 episodes of a cartoon, "Mr. Magoo." Jim Backus was the voice of this stumpy, half blind old dimwit that carried on a nonstop boring monologue. Mr Magoo unknowingly faced many perils and made all the wrong decisions but by the grace of God never came to any harm. Such episodes as <u>Matador Magoo</u>, <u>Magoo Goes Skiing</u>, <u>Magoos Canine</u> <u>Mutiny</u>, and my personal favorite <u>Merry Minstrel Magoo</u> hint at the potential dangers that could befall a vulnerable old man. Yet he rose unscathed much like magoogled drunks who have a halo above and a charm in their pocket. If you are going to be drunk you can only hope to be in this very blessed state of magooledness.

"What's your all time favorite cartoon?"

"Bugs Bunny.
A nice tail and
strong teeth are
very attractive to
a girl."

UPHOLSTERED:

Is of a Jewish origin also born out of Depression heartaches. The beautiful Pocono Mountains in upstate New York was home to a vibrant Jewish community consisting of many economic tiers. The wealthy depended on the tradesmen to repair and restore their valuable possessions, priceless furniture being a part thereof. After a long trek to the Master's house, stuffing, stretching, beating and tacking the furniture then haggling prices the old Jew upholsterer would return worse for wear to his wife but not before stopping for a little sustenance at a nearby pub in order to restore his resolve for tomorrow. Being of a frugal nature the old Jew reasoned he might in one visit restore his resolve for an entire week by drinking his pro-rata share that very evening. This wisdom was not nurtured by his wife who upon his unsteady arrival home began upholstering the old Jew about the upper torso. It was a sad day in that present but a rare comic refrain of Jewish lore when of the past.

CRISPY:

Is not actually a word that portrays drunkenness but the delicate and fleeting state just afore the loss of sobriety. This adjective obviously emanated from an observant person while frying bacon. One can remove bacon from the skillet yet it will continue to cook for some time thereafter only to exhibit a burnt exterior not unlike a person who thinks she has stopped drinking in time yet continues to enter unwillingly into intemperance.

ALL IN A HEAP:

The operative word is heap which likely represents either the look your hair takes on as it lies about your head or the look of your clothes as it wads and gathers around your broken body. If you are All in a Heap it is likely your appearance is fodder for many witty and sneering slurs from otherwise courteous guests.

"Getting drunk is a big waste of time."

"In life I never waste my time although I often dawdle on the good parts."

SPIFFICATED:

Is an actual word that means out of sync with one's surroundings but its use depicting a less than sober state originated from the men's restroom of the Waldorf Astoria some sixty years ago. You see back then restrooms had attendants who would brush your suit, wipe your shoes etc. upon exiting the toilet. I can't imagine why one required those services at that particular moment but it seems a very keen attendant, Samuel Etheridge, was greatly amused by the varied ways a drunk gentleman would try to pull himself together before meeting the outside world again. He concluded a man was spifficatedly drunk when he attempted to act spiffy and sophisticated in order to hide his impious state. Additionally Mr. Etheridge observed men who were, as he called them stocious, trying to act stoic as a maneuver to pretend righteousness. Often stocious drunks, as witnessed by Etheridge, were mistaken for stoned drunks which helped their cause not an iota.

SCUPPERED:

Is an old English nautical term that arose from an incident involving a ship's cook, the skipper and his supper. Without delving too deeply into the darker realities of 18th century discipline(or pleasure as the case may be) I must just say that little Willie Mann, the cook on the ship "Quadriga" conspired over some several weeks in lifting for his personal consumption the ship's very best victuals to the gastronomical detriment of the ship's captain, Sir John Forrester. Finger screws and pliers allowed a speedy confession. Being of a soft and compliant nature Capt. John gave poor Willie access to the ship's store of rum of which he made ample use so as to assuage the lashes that were to be administered upon his bare back that very evening. It would have worked too except upon seeing the now totally smashed little Willie, laughing brashly and exhibiting little remorse for his thievery being led in handcuffs to the flogging pole, the righteous and I might venture to say impetuous Capt. John Forrester instead hurled the poor cook overboard forthwith. Scuppered characterizes a drunken person who through rude behavior lowers any possible benevolent feelings others might patiently bestow on "Scuppy" to his possible disadvantage.

"Why is it when you're nicely tied to a bedpost everything starts to itch?"

"I'm good but not gaudy: well, not overly gaudy."

Two Sided Compliments

You have successfully slogged through to the last chapter. Congratulations, I finished two chapters ago.

"If I finish early I just start over again."

Actually the need for this last chapter is bittersweet. Since you are now so adroitly trained about wine in general and choosing wine specifically you should never have distasteful wine around the house, right? Wrong. We all usually end up with unwanted wine through well intended gifts from friends and relatives who are ignorant of the advice contained in this book.

There are two solutions. Rid yourself of these "ignorant" friends and estrange yourself from family or give them a copy of "Laughing at Wine."

Until this menacing problem is eradicated your response upon being given a bottle of distasteful goop is crucial. Picture yourself hosting a dinner party and these uninformed guests show up and present you a bottle of pomace. Whatever are you to do? It is only human nature in moments like these to over thank them because you fear you're disgust might show through. This little quirk in manners only encourages them to continue this foul habit, a habit that must be nipped in the bud.

We accomplish this feat with what I call "two sided compliments." These are responses that exhibit your genteel manners yet subtly convey the message that you really don't want to witness this rot gut ever again. Below is a list of two sided compliments you're free to use. They work on most ignorant guests. I've used them.

TWO SIDED COMPLIMENT

*You shouldn't have. No, I mean it. You really shouldn't have.

"Shouldn't is a contraction I seldom utter, particularly when I'm about to have one."

*Oh how sweet. My Grandmother drank a glass of this very wine at bedtime for medicinal purposes.

*Oh how wonderful. This will go well with food we seldom serve.

*Oh how wonderful. My husband will love this wine, he drinks Budweiser cans.

*Oh you dear. This looks like the kind of wine you could just leave in the bag and drink straight from the bottle.

*Oh, how environmentally conscience you are. Corks are becoming scarce anyway.

*How did you know? We just built a wine cellar and have just the place to STUFF this one.

*How did you ever know I drank this wine in college when I needed a cheap drunk.

*Oh how interesting. You'll have to tell me more about the vineyard that grows pink grapes.

*How delightful. My husband recently suggested I drink strange wines from countries I never heard of. And I thought he was being facetious.

*Perfect timing. Jim's alcoholic sister is visiting us tomorrow. This should slow her down.

*Oh how sweet, I'll make certain you get it at dinner.

*How wonderful. Now I know what to serve after everyone gets drunk.

*Oh, you must know I have a wonderful sense of humor.

*Oh, this one would have been just right if only we were serving bratwurst and sauerkraut.

*Lovely, lovely. But you must have kept the two little plastic glasses that came with it.

*Oh how thoughtful. Hopefully you didn't waste much time choosing this one.

*Oh this is an interesting one. Wasn't it recommended in True Crime Magazine?

*This one might actually serve a purpose. Which dinner guest do you abhor?

*You are a dear. Jim and I needed a reason to pare down our drinking. This should do it.

*Thanks dear. Our Rottweiler loves you.

*Wonderful. Such a natural wine. Look at all the sediment in the bottom.

*I can't imagine what you were thinking when you bought this one. What in fact were you thinking? Were you thinking?

"For me trying to think about what I was thinking is double jeopardy."

*You're so cute. You must read National Inquirer too?

*Right on. I needed some cooking wine.

*Oh you dear. Doesn't regifting make attending dinner parties less expensive?

*How sweet. What, no sardines?

*Oh this will come in handy when anyone in the house suffers from irregularity.

*Well this one is interesting. I'll store it in the medicine cabinet with the rest of the cough syrup.

You get the idea. Write us about "two sided compliments" that have worked for you.

OK, so we've done just about everything to keep distasteful wine from our cupboards yet invariably even in the most respected households bad wine may occasionally reside. So whatever are we to do other than regift and cook with them? This is my creative challenge to you.

You may often complain of a lack of creative talent. So what if you can't paint, sing or fiddle, or pole dance. You now have an opportunity to delve into your gray matter and allow those juices to flow. Think outside of the box and write me creative ways to use unwanted wine.

I'll start with a few of my own "creative uses of bad wine."

*Add a tablespoon of vinegar to wine. Retrieve turquoise crayon from your child's toy box and faintly color one side of the cork. Return bottle to retailer in exchange for a better varietal.

*There are two groups of people that temporarily lose their palate in lieu of just wanting alcohol. Stress does that to a person. Distasteful wine will not go to waste if given to either a recently divorced woman or to the mother of an active three year old boy. If the woman in question is recently divorced and has an active three year old boy , there is no pomace bad enough that can't find a welcome home. I don't suggest you show up on a stranger's doorstep bottle in hand just because you read in the local rag she is recently divorced or has young children but it is wise to be abreast of your social surroundings in order to seize upon these opportunities when available.

*Several years ago we added a large concrete patio to our home. We paid the contractor to not only stamp the concrete with a design but add coloring as well. The stamping worked but the coloring didn't, leaving us with a rather stark look to the place. Not until a guest dropped his glass of red wine did it occur to me that a unique modeled maroon design can be formatted on the patio using unwanted burgundy. It's ever changing, a work in progress you might say.

*If you are lucky enough to have grown children rather than the less desirable just children you likely have an outlet for the sweeter unwanted varietals.

*Revenge and unwanted wines are natural companions. Distasteful wines can be administered to people who reside at the bottom of your warm and fuzzy list.

*Wine snobs are highly susceptible to trickery. Pouring cheap wine in empty expensive wine bottles works some interesting magic at times. The real challenge is remaining stoic while the snob professes his ability to distinguish the complex and subtle nuances of this very elegant wine.

*At your dinner party certain people tend to stay beyond their welcome and need to be encouraged to irritate people in their own homes rather than yours. This is easily accomplished by handing them a full glass of your worst goop. I simply look upon this as a form of crowd control.

"I'm near breathless
waiting for your ideas.

"The greatest miracle on earth is a yellow duck."

Epilogue

Don't know what an epilogue is really, but most classy books have one. So in my eternal struggle to pretend to be something I'm not qualified to be I'm including an epilogue.

Actually an epilogue reminds me of a eulogy in a way. You sum up a life, tell all the good and funny stories then close the casket with only memories remaining.

Your memory of this book is important to me. You can't possibly forget Darla who reminds us that with self esteem life is a carnival. And poor Lloyd exudes imperfection. They both illustrate how fallible and pathetic we are, particularly the rich. Yet Darla and Lloyd are happy because they love themselves. Not narcissistic love but accepting love. They have acquired, by some unimaginable means, a good dose of self worth.

So, may I suggest you sit back with one glass of wine every evening, tell yourself you're doing the best you can (even though that in itself is a lie), and make a loving toast to yourself, and

LAUGH.

Postscript

Dear reader, thanks for taking a walk with Darla, Lloyd and me down insanity lane. We had a blast. I've never accomplished a worthwhile goal unless I could laugh at it first.

Darla says "everyone is a joke looking for a punch line." Hopefully you've found a few punch lines for you and your friends in this tawdry little book.

I encourage you to visit our website www.laughingatwine.com for some additional entertainment and gifts. You can write us your funny drinking stories, incidents, definitions etc. We will post a new one weekly and eventually publish some of them in our next book.

Because Darla is trashy she insists on classy gifts. So as the months proceed we will notify you of giftware we've added to our site. They will be unique, economical and bring a little laughter to your soul.

Adieu,   jerry morris